Mabel's Miraculous Manner

Stories of Kindness and Friendship

by
Frank English
and his apprentice writers from
St Luke's CE Primary School, Lancaster

First Edition published 2022 by
2QT Limited (Publishing)
Settle, North Yorkshire BD24 9BZ United Kingdom

Copyright © Frank English 2022
The right of Frank English to be identified as the authors of this work has been asserted by him/her in accordance with the Copyright, Designs and Patents Act 1988

All rights reserved. This book is sold subject to the condition that no part of this book is to be reproduced, in any shape or form. Or by way of trade, stored in a retrieval system or transmitted in any form or by any means, electronic, mechanical, photocopying, recording, be lent, re-sold, hired out or otherwise circulated in any form of binding or cover other than that in which it is published and without a similar condition, including this condition being imposed on the subsequent purchaser, without prior permission of the copyright holder.

The author has his own website: https://www.frankenglish.co.uk/
Cover Illustration by Ian R Ward,
from a drawing by eleven-year-old Eden Phillips

Printed in Great Britain by
Ingram Sparks

A CIP catalogue record for this book is available
from the British Library
ISBN - 978-1-914083-70-9

After the huge success of ***Josephine's Journey*** (created by twelve Year 6 apprentice writers) and ***Garnett's Grand Getaway*** (by a full class of twenty-nine) at Skerton St Luke's, Lancaster, Frank and I, with the help of six Year 6 children, decided to take the writing experience one step further. We decided to introduce the story writing and publishing journey to *all* ages at St Luke's.

The truly amazing thing about the children at St Luke's is their imagination, their creativity, and their awe and wonder. All of this starts at the very beginning of their St Luke's journey in Reception and then continues throughout the full seven years until the last moment when they sadly leave to start their next chapter, in secondary school.

We believe that they are the authors of their own learning, and we certainly advocate *that* throughout the school with the passion of all our amazing staff members.

We are proud to be a ***Reading School*** at St Luke's.

Since our return to school after the tragic pandemic, our children have amazed us with their passion and enjoyment of sharing, drafting, writing and editing their own stories. Consequently, it seemed the most perfect timing to involve the entire school in the writing and publishing of this fantastically imaginative story for a more public stage.

Each class worked eagerly with Frank English in the summer term to create a main character and a storyline that were linked to one of our school values. This overall story is also a true reflection of our school ethos as in Luke 10:27, *'Love your neighbour as yourself'*.

The initial conversations and the thought-provoking idea of the whole school being involved was actually generated by six wonderful Year 6 apprentice authors who wanted to create a story about a very special person. Sadly, Patricia Swarbrick passed away in 2020. A devoted and loving wife, mother, nana and great-nana, it seemed right that this story should be dedicated to her in loving memory.

Frank was honoured to be asked by these children to craft the final kind, meaningful story from their ideas, storylines and incredible joint imagination. The rest, as they say, is history . . .

Here we have it . . .

Mabel's Miraculous Manner

Miss Garnett
Assistant Head and Year 6 Class Teacher

Reception

Reception – Class of 2021/22

Elsie B Faith J Georgia G Jack S

Phoebe S Steven C Una N Molly K

Alex F Mrs Goodwin Dylan C

Miss Grime Miss Cokell Mrs Stanborough

Signatures

Georgia Oscar

Alex

Amy Elsie Leo

Molly

Dylan Darcie Ellse

Josie

Leah-marie Josh

Jack Chloe

Faith Phoebe

Una Annie Josie Vovi

Chapter 1

'Oh no!' the little green and pink spotted caterpillar muttered once she had managed to squeeze herself out of the hard little egg that was still sticking to the dark green foliage above her.

She crawled behind two large leaves as she looked out onto the new world she had never seen before. What she saw made no sense at all to her. A bright yellow light shone into her face and made her close her delicate little eyes in pain.

'I . . . don't . . . like . . . this . . . place!' she struggled to say, as an enormous creature landed on a branch close by, shaking the twigs but making her remain silent and still, in fear.

'I can't see any of those wriggly little creatures!' a tiny bird chirruped as it searched for its first meal of the day.

'Try looking a little closer,' his mama urged, trying to get him to find his own food for the first time since his feathers had grown to allow him to flit around in search. 'There are lots of them about.'

Fortunately for the little caterpillar, the baby bird wasn't very good at moving twigs or hopping about on the branches and among the leaves that hid his food. His mama hopped onto the next branch and moved a leaf to show him where other little green-and-pink-spotted wriggly caterpillars were hiding, all afraid of the mama bird's sharp beak.

'See?' she chirruped patiently. 'Here they are. Come and try one before they all wriggle to the edge and fall to the floor.'

As the little bird moved slowly along the twig to choose his meal, he stopped sharply, his eyes opening wide with surprise and more than a little fear.

Beneath the branch they were sitting on, a young girl had stopped to look up at the birds as they crept about among the leaves looking for a meal.

'Look, Mummy!' the little girl said as she pointed upwards in excitement. The birds took off in fear and the caterpillars stopped wriggling, hoping they wouldn't be seen.

A delicate but exciting voice poured over the frightened little caterpillar. 'Hello,' it said.

She looked around slowly and carefully, barely daring to move her head too quickly for fear of being seen.

'Up here,' the new voice encouraged, trying to make her feel brave enough to look up. 'No need to be afraid. I am as *you* will be in a little while. You have no need to fear me. Look up. Please?'

Slowly, carefully, gaining in courage little by little as the new voice's kindness began to encourage her confidence to grow, she turned around. She looked upwards, and an amazed gasp escaped from her tiny mouth. There, hovering above her, almost stationary in the air except for the gentle movement of her startlingly wonderful wings, was a gloriously beautiful butterfly.

'What – who – are . . . you?' the tiny green-and-pink-spotted caterpillar gasped, almost unable to believe what she saw above her. 'I . . . have . . . never . . . seen—'

'A butterfly that once looked very much like . . . you?' the butterfly answered.

'I don't unders . . . undist . . . underst . . . know what you mean,' the caterpillar replied, now standing as tall as she was able on her four rear legs.

'You and I are . . . cousins,' the butterfly added quietly. 'We came from the same family, and one day, not far away, *you* will look like . . . *me*.'

The caterpillar was stunned into silence, unable to understand or believe what the butterfly was saying. 'You mean that—?' the caterpillar gasped.

'One day you will change from your green-and-pink-spotted body—' she explained.

'Into a wonderful creature with . . . flappy things that will make me able to move around not on the ground and—' the caterpillar said.

'Be free and able to escape those other creatures that want to eat you,' the butterfly said. 'By the way, my name is Patty.'

'Oo, I like the sound of that!' the caterpillar said, a little easier and with more confidence than a few moments earlier. 'Will I be able—?'

'To fly like me?' Patty answered kindly. 'Yes. You will. Almost exactly like me.'

'I like your . . .' the caterpillar added, a curious look on her face.

'Name?' Patty answered.

'Patty . . .' Caterpillar repeated slowly as she settled back onto her eight legs on the twig. 'I think I would like to be called . . . Fatty.'

'Doesn't work like that,' Patty said, a butterfly sort of a smile on her face. 'That name would mean that you would be much larger than you should be. How about . . . Hatty?'

'I like it! I like it!' Caterpillar Hatty said, turning around much too quickly and falling over as she did so.

'Hatty! Hatty! Hatty!' Caterpillar Hatty sang joyfully. 'Now I know who I am. Thank you for your kindness, Patty. I . . .'

Patty was no longer there. Seeing her new friend gain in confidence because of *her* kindness was all she needed. Hopefully, Hatty would grow even more and do the same for some other unconfident and fearful newly hatched green-and-pink-spotted caterpillar, or even one that was dark brown and hairy!

Year 1

Year 1 - Class of 2021/22

Vanda J   Bella R   Olivia W   Rosie S

Eliza D   Holly R   Evelyn W   Bella- Rae S

Marshall H   Evie H   Arabelle R   Poppy C

Mrs Busby   Miss Race   Miss Bartholomew

Signatures

Emily
Izzy
Olivia

Matthew
Jack

Leah Alfie
Lee Rosie Evlin le
        Bella   vanda
  Kayden   Seb Arabelle
   Eliza Holly
   Amber   Ollie
     Evie
        Mateusz   Austin
  Alex Dominick
   Mason

Chapter 2

'Oh dear! Oh dear!' Mabel the slow-moving baby tortoise muttered as she hurried home to her mama for tea. She had been able to taste those delicious dandelion leaves and glorious yellow flowers ever since she had set off early that morning to stumble to the huge patch she had been told about. 'I'm going to be late, and Mama will not be pleased!'

She tended to mutter to herself a lot, mainly because she was so slow that all the companions who had set off with her had become so fed up with waiting for her that they had usually left her after the first dozen or so steps.

She had, of course, become so lonely that she had accepted that situation, knowing she would always be much slower than any other animal in the wild. Oh, how she wished she hadn't been born such a slow-moving creature!

'How did I know that most of the dandelions would have been eaten before I got there?' she sighed, as she slowed to take a well-needed rest under a dense hawthorn bush at the edge of a dark and spooky wood. 'Woah! I don't remember *this* wood on the way out! Has it just grown as I have been walking? Or . . . have I taken the wrong . . . path . . . again?'

She stopped, extending her concertina-like neck to try to gain her bearings, only to be almost poked in the eye by a near-invisible young twig. Although slow in every other way, she had been blessed with very fastblinking eyelids. This made her realise that she already knew this wood.

'Phew!' she gasped. 'That was a close shave. Now what am I going to do? There is no way I am going to get home before . . . tomorrow. What would my friend Alice say if she were here?

'She would advise me to make myself comfortable under this bush and have a nap until—' she mumbled slowly, as sleep gently closed her eyes once her flexible neck had drawn her head into her carapace. Clever creatures, those tortoises! Always automatically drawing in their sticking-out bits to stop them from being bitten off by some extremely hungry much larger creature that loved the taste of tortoise.

Unfortunately, *this* little tortoise always had a very vivid dream time the moment she fell into an almost immediate deep slumber. Usually, she was either attacked by a larger creature that fancied a tortoise sandwich or she was whisked away to some scary place she had never seen before.

As she began to wake up slowly, a very strong smell of smoke forced its way into her nostrils and made her cough and sneeze enough to realise that she felt very warm and unable to see further than the end of her carapace.

'What—?' she muttered as her neck stretched beyond her shell to see what was happening.

'It's a fire,' a quietly cooing voice told her.

'A . . . fire?' Mabel asked. 'What's a . . . fire?'

'Everything's burning around us,' the cooing creature continued. 'If we don't move quickly, we will be burned with everything else.'

'Who or what are *you*?' the tortoise asked, yawning as she stretched her neck and her legs. She opened her eyes wide to see a feathery creature with a curved but pointy beak, only two thin spindly legs, and a fat body with two wings. One of the wings was hanging down by his side. 'What's the matter with your wing?'

'He is a pigeon, and he has injured it,' another, much lighter, voice interrupted.

Both Mabel and the pigeon looked around in surprise, to find a beautifully delicate creature sitting on a twig, her colourful wings folded back, with what seemed to be a smile on her face.

'You are a—' the pigeon cooed quietly.

'Butterfly,' the creature said. 'My name is Patty. I know both *your* names.'

'How . . . ?' both animals asked, puzzled as to how that might be possible.

'And why am I here with all these funny-looking big trees, when I went to sleep under my usual safe bush in *my* forest?' Mabel the little tortoise asked. 'Why have they got no leaves or . . . or . . . branches?'

'That's because they are buildings,' Patty answered. 'Buildings that humans live in. Your next questions are going to ask why there is a lot of smoke, why you can't see very well and why it is so hot.'

Mabel gasped. She had never come across such a smart creature before. In fact, she had never met *any* other creatures before, except for her mama and one or two companions who never seemed to be there when she needed them. But that's another story.

'We have two problems,' Patty went on. 'The first one is that Samuel Pepys here has injured his wing—'

'Singed the feathers, actually, in that black and white building over there,' Pepys explained. 'I was just minding my own business and looking for breakfast, when—'

'And secondly, he needs something to take away the pain, to let him fly again,' Patty went on, ignoring the pigeon's interruption.

'But why black and white . . . buildings – whatever they are? And why does the cloudy stuff make my throat want to cough and be sick?' Mabel asked, still confused about where she was. 'Where *are* we?'

'This is a very big town where lots of humans live. It is called Lon Don,' Patty explained. 'That fire you can see has been burning for nearly four days, destroying all it touches.'

'How have I got here, when all I remember is having a nap under one of my favourite hawthorn bushes only what seems to have been a few moments ago?' Mabel puzzled in disbelief. 'How—?'

'As far as I am aware, my dear Mabel, you are the only one hereabouts that knows how to make Samuel Pepys's wing better by—' Patty went on patiently.

'Using aloe vera?' Mabel burst out, surprising herself. 'I know where there is some of that . . . I think. I love its taste and feel as it goes down—'

'*Now* would be a good time,' Patty urged, patient as ever.

Mabel set off very slowly, her neck fully extended, snuffling to left and right, trying to find the scent of her plant in this very unfamiliar place in what felt like a very long time ago.

Suddenly, she stopped, one of her front legs raised just above the soil outside of a dense clump of strange-looking plants. Slowly she approached the clump, sniffing the air all the while. Within a whisker of the first plant, she nibbled the outside sword-shaped stem gingerly, taking its tip into her mouth.

'Cung 'ere!' she muttered, unable to move her mouth to say the words properly.

Fortunately, Pepys understood without difficulty and, stretching out his wing, he stumbled towards the tortoise. Closing her mouth gently around the plant's stalk, Mabel squeezed some of the green-coloured juice onto Samuel Pepys's injured wing, just as darkness closed about them.

'My goodness!' Mabel muttered as she opened her eyes on the twigs and leaves of the hawthorn bush she had fallen asleep under. 'What a strange dream. Can't believe . . .'

Catching the narrow bright-yellow rays of morning sunlight as they pierced the gloom surrounding her, she looked up from the bush to see a lone pigeon cooing soothingly on a branch just above her head. One of his wings seemed to be a little strangely shaped and different from the other.

'Hello,' the pigeon cooed.

'Who are you, and why are you staring at me?' Mabel asked, a little sharply.

'My name is Samuel Pepys,' the pigeon replied quietly, 'and I owe you my deepest thanks for the help you have given me.'

'Samuel Pepys? Thanks?' the little tortoise said as she stood still, in shock, unable to believe what perhaps had just happened.

Year 2

Year 2 – Class of 2021/22

Pippa M

Melody C-J

Marvel M-H

Emmie F C

David R

Martha C

Zachary H

Vinnie D-E

Amelia B

Amber H

Lilly K

Archie H

Matilda P

Halle L

Connie R

Jacob C

Poppy C | Molly K | Daisy S | Calvin R

Emma J | Gracie T | Connie W | Josh S

Henry P | Michael L | Isla S | Lily-Mae P

Mr Andrew | Emily B | Mrs Plevey

Signatures

Isla   Jacob   michael
                                molly
  nlass   Emmie   Emma
                                Merry
                                Martha
David   Amber
Joshua
            Connie   Halle
Calvin   Archie   Pippa Lilly K
         Zoe Vinnie
          Mary   Poppy
                                Matilda
     Daisy

    Gracie-T   Marvel   Amelia-B
    Connier

  Lily Mae   Emily

26

Chapter 3

Sally the salamander didn't like winter. To be truthful, she wasn't keen on spring or autumn either. She was able to tolerate summer only when the sun reached its closest to her stretch of the world, and even then it only did so very infrequently. Her favourite time was when the wild country she lived in became very dry through lack of rain and burst into flames. *Then* she was happy.

Unfortunately, it seemed to be getting wetter as time rolled on, which meant she was always cold.

She had thought often about setting fire to her woods to allow her to become warmer. Those yellow and red tongues of flames licking around her and through her habitat were wonderful thoughts that she wished she could make happen. The problem was that she didn't know *how* to make it happen.

She didn't have many friends, because they were afraid that *she* might burst into flames at a moment's notice. She wouldn't ever have done that, of course, because she liked flames close enough to her to make her warm, but not so close that she might become burned.

Her big problem was that she was a cold-blooded creature whose bodily fluids never became warm naturally unless she was able to bask in the very warm sunshine that many parts of the world had on a regular basis. Unfortunately for her, she didn't live in any of *those* places. The very few creatures she was able to call friends *were* warm-blooded, and they thought it was a marvel that she could survive at all, so they called her Marvellous Manda.

An early snowfall had dropped the temperature very close to freezing overnight, persuading Sally to find shelter urgently. Shuffling along an already frozen path into the oak forest, close to a clearing where she usually spent most of her time trying to find the sun, she suddenly skidded sideways on an icy patch. Unable to keep her balance, she tipped over a rocky outcrop into a small cave, injuring one of her back legs as she fell.

A startled voice from the back of the cave greeted the salamander. 'Goodness gracious me! Who on earth are *you*? I wasn't expecting visitors at this time of day, and certainly not a—'

'My name is Sally and I am a . . . salamander,' Sally gasped as she slithered to a halt not two swishes of her tail from a creature she had never seen before. The look of surprised shock on her face was enough to prompt the cave's occupant to speak.

'You are probably wondering who and what I am, and why I'm in this cave,' the creature said. 'My name is Garnett and I am a . . . tortoise. I am in here because – like you, I guess – I am not able to warm up my body without sitting close to heat or without moving to somewhere warmer outside.'

'It certainly is somewhat warmer in here, I am pleased to say,' Sally agreed.

'Are you in here . . . ?' Garnett asked.

'By accident, really,' Sally said as she explained what had happened. 'And I think I've injured my back leg.'

She sat down with a bump and looked around the cave. A certain amount of light crept in through the entrance, where a large overhang and several big tree roots prevented snow from joining them. It was dry, much warmer than outside, and there was a good amount of dry straw and small twigs that might be used to make a fire.

'The way you are looking at the straw and wood, I think you might be wondering if we could make a fire,' Garnett said. 'We could if we had something to light it with. You can probably see the small hole in the roof way up there, so smoke wouldn't be a problem. But—'

'Perhaps I might help with that,' a softer, kinder voice butted in. This caused both cold-blooded creatures to turn around sharply, to catch sight of a very unexpected creature that was perched on a long twig close to the pile of straw.

'And you are . . . ?' Garnett asked very pointedly, not sure what sort of a creature they were dealing with.

'My name is Patty, and I am a butterfly,' the vividly coloured creature explained as she spread her glorious wings.

'So, you are about to magic fire into our little shelter, then?'

Garnett suggested, a slight sneer curling the corners of her mouth.

'Not really,' the butterfly explained. 'If you look to the very back corner of the cave, you will see and feel *real* heat coming from underground. If you build a wall of straw around it with space enough for the two of you to sit, you will have enough heat to warm your bodies for quite some time.'

'Where is it coming from?' Sally asked, unsure of the magic of it all.

'All I know is that it's coming from underground and will provide warmth for all of us until it becomes much less cold outside,' Patty replied. 'Your next question, I am sure, will be about . . . food. There are plenty of worms, woodlice, maggots and snails in the corner for you, Sally, and dandelions in flower further over for you, Garnett. That should keep you both going for quite some time, I think.'

Following Patty's very sensible suggestion, Garnett and Sally set to, pushing straw out of the corners of the cave to allow a good deal of heat to come into the cave, where they built a thick straw wall and laid a deep carpet of dry straw to keep their feet warm, too.

'You can rest your sore leg now, as well, Marvellous Manda, for the next few days to allow it to heal,' Garnett suggested, pleased with what they had achieved. 'Plenty of food, I think, for both of us.'

'What about you, Patty Butterfly?' the salamander asked, concerned their helpful host might starve for lack of something delicious to eat. 'Patty? What would *you* like to eat?'

Turning around because of Patty's silence, they noticed that she was no longer there.

'Where's she gone?' the tortoise asked, looking around again, puzzled how such a delicate creature could have just . . . disappeared. Was she real, or just something they had imagined?

Year 3

Year 3 – Class of 2021/22

 Tyler A
 Bessie B
 Joseph R
 Poppy-Marie F

 Joe A
 Arya T
 Amelia B
 Sam B

 Jack P
 Ellie-Rae H
 Caitlin B
 Preston K

 Mrs Heywood / Mrs Billington
 Jayden F
 Sapphire C
 Mrs Holroyd

Signatures

Nibl

Scarlet

Daisy

Ben

Joseph T

Evie

Ellie

Renae

Bessi

Sam

Jack P

Jessica W

Eve

Jayden

Poppy

Sapphire

Caitlin

Amelia

Maddie

Joseph-Rogers

Tyler

Anya

Preston

George

Aidan

Joe A

Jessica - A

Finley

Rose

Chapter 4

Farmer Borril's field, where he cultivated millions of carrots for the whole of the town in which he lived, was enormous and very well known by many, including a large population of very hungry and extremely greedy rabbits.

Several times a day, they gathered just outside the three holes to their burrows at the edge of the field, close to a deep, clear stream that chuckled over and around many large boulders along its swirling length. Eventually it disappeared into a shady wood of stout oak and beech and birch trees. This wood, it was said by the local people who lived in the small nearby town, was spooky and ghostly, and not a place to visit on your own . . . at any time. Some of the hardier rabbits, however, had excavated comfortable burrows within its eaves, allowing them to raid this wonderful carrot pantry under cover at any time.

Unfortunately, unbeknown to this group of fat, greedy rabbits, a family of foxes had moved into and extended a disused burrow quite close by. It wasn't long before *they* discovered their good luck at having a pantry of their *own* closer to home than they had ever had before. Carrots aplenty? No fear! *Their* minds were *not* set on vegetables! Never had been – never would be.

Bruno the young rabbit was very innocent about the world about him and discovered very early in his short life how wonderfully full Farmer Borril's carrots made him feel. He loved living on the edge of *that* particular field, where he had the chance to nibble whenever he felt the need growing inside him. Little did he know that occasionally he was being watched from a little hill close to the stream.

The creature watching him was a young tortoise called Mabel. On a number of occasions she had left her little hill to amble, very slowly, to try to meet Bruno, because she thought he might make a good friend. She had no friends who were tortoises, because they all thought she was very slow, even for a tortoise, and she didn't like the dark.

She often wondered what relevance that might have for a tortoise, but they never stayed long enough in her company for her to find out. Therefore, she had become a very lonely tortoise who would try very hard to find and keep at least one friend. Could Bruno be that one?

Although rabbits were supposed to be very quick so they could escape any predator that might like to have such animals for lunch, Bruno either liked to take his time or he was one of the slowest of his kind. This is what had attracted Mabel to him as a friend.

This particular morning, Mabel had woken after a poor night to dark clouds scudding across the sky, which were not allowing the summer sun to make much of an appearance. Occasional brief flashes of sunshine winked through the gaps in the clouds, making all creatures think that it was going to be a lovely day, only to have their hopes dashed moments later.

During one of these brief spells of hope, Mabel decided to visit the possible friend she could see sitting on his haunches with a carrot top sticking out of the side of his mouth. This was going to be her day, she felt sure. Upon leaving the protection of the last mighty oak tree behind, once she had nibbled an acorn or two before she stumbled into the carrot field, she could see no rabbit anywhere.

'Drat and double . . . drat!' she muttered, disappointment ringing in her voice. 'I could have sworn—'

'Help!' A very quiet but panic-stricken voice seemed to draw her attention. She stopped to listen, her fully stretched neck waving slowly from side to side as she tried to locate the sound.

'Must have been the wind,' she muttered again, dismissing what she thought she had heard.

She had seen where all the rabbit holes were when the occupants of all the family burrows had come out for dinner or breakfast, so she thought it a good idea to visit each hole and have a sit down to wait.

As she approached the first hole, she stopped sharply. Although she thought she knew where it was, she couldn't find it anywhere.

'Where on earth . . . ?' she puzzled. 'I'm sure it should be . . . here.'

'Help me!' she heard again, louder this time – almost directly beneath her shell.

Looking around again, more closely this time, she noticed that one of the holes had what seemed like a fuzzy plant growing out of it. Reaching over to give it a tug with her hard beak-like mouth, a squeaking 'Ouch! Help! Oh no! Ouch . . . ouch . . . ouch!' made her realise very quickly that what she was trying to pluck was a rabbit's scut!

'Hello?' Mabel gasped. 'Who's that? Are you a . . . rabbit?'

'Yes! Yes! Yes!' an urgent, muffled squeak squeezed out of the hole. 'I am Bruno, and I am . . . stuck. Could you get me out, please?'

'Pull you out?' Mabel replied in shock. 'And how do you expect me to do that? You weren't so keen on my pulling your tail a moment ago.'

'Push?' Bruno mumbled. 'From below?'

'So you'd like me to dig a hole?' Mabel asked sarcastically. 'I am a tortoise with four legs, no claws, and a heavy shell to bear, and I . . . do . . . not . . . like . . . the dark!'

'Yef pleave,' Bruno muttered. 'I don't like being squeezed in dis tight plafe. It makes me feel I'm fastened in.'

A similar voice moved into their conversation. 'Yes, Barry, it is!'

'No, Harry, it's not!' another replied. 'Why would it be him? That's somebody *else's* scut.'

Mabel turned to face the other two rabbits that had popped out of another rabbit hole close by that she hadn't seen before.

'And who might you be?' Mabel asked sharply. 'Are you anything to do with this youngster here?'

'He's our brother, we think, by the sound of his voice,' Harry said.

'It looks like his backside, too,' Barry added. 'You can't miss that anywhere.'

'Anyway, he's stuck,' Mabel said.

'Probably because he eats too much,' Harry said, 'and that makes him too fat to use this particular hole.'

'His overweightness makes him forgetful as well,' Barry butted in.

'Forgetful?' Mabel queried. 'How do you make that one out?'

'He tends to forget that this is the only hole he gets stuck in when he's had too much to eat,' Harry said with a grin.

Throughout this toing and froing, a startlingly colourful butterfly alighted on the trumpet of a large yellow flower, hoping that she wouldn't have to encourage the rabbits and tortoise to take action to rescue the young rabbit from being stuck between worlds.

'We can't leave him there,' Mabel insisted. 'He might . . . die.'

The two young rabbits laughed at each other as they turned to leave.

'Oh no you don't!' Mabel shouted at Harry as she took hold

of his brother's hind leg in her strong and sharp beak. 'If you don't help your brother Bruno, I will bite off this leg, and then where will you be?'

'A three-legged rabbit?' Harry sniggered.

'All right! All right!' Barry shouted. 'Down into the hole, Harry, old chap, and get a few other brothers to help you push him out. Then we can all go home for tea.'

With a smile on her face, Patty the butterfly lifted off from the flower and fluttered away to the strange sound of the rabbits singing,

'Heave ho, mi hearties!

Push! Push! And plop him out.'

This left Mabel trying to draw in her neck and head to cut out this strangely, gurglingly awful sound of rabbits in song, although she couldn't wait to see what Bruno looked like face to face.

Chapter 5

Poppy the young fox sat quietly in her comfortable hollow under a dense bramble bush. Her mama and papa called to see her regularly to make sure she was safe and well, and still . . . there. They often tried to persuade her to join them in one of their earths or dens close by, but she always refused. Her parents, or one or two other adults from earlier litters, often took her food or scraps to eat to make sure she didn't go without, but she had always refused, politely, to leave her safe place.

'Why do you think our Poppy won't leave her hiding place, Horace?' Mama Fox asked her husband, knowing what his answer was likely to be.

'I put it down to one of two things, really,' he replied, very sure of himself.

'And the first thing is?' she said with a resigned sigh.

'She doesn't like the dark . . . at all,' he explained in his usual sure way. 'She never has, and I assume she never will, unless divine intervention says otherwise.'

'And the second reason?' Mama asked as she settled down to suckle her new brood.

'She is not overly keen on . . . sunlight, either,' he said, after a deep sigh and a moment's thought. 'The worst of all worlds, I think.'

'That means she will never live a normal foxy life!' Mama insisted. 'This has never happened before, certainly in our world, and if our other – older – children hadn't decided to help, she wouldn't have survived, particularly in the winter that can be quite challenging. We are now into June, and the colder months are not far away. Can't you do *anything*?'

'What? Like dragging her out when we hunt? Breaking down her little den?' he suggested. 'She would leave the area to find somewhere else to live, and we would never see her again – alive.'

'The problem is that she has no friends to share her life with,' Mama said, after a moment or two's thought. 'If she had—'

'We wouldn't need to worry too much about her,' Pappa Fox interrupted, 'and she would be normal, with a family of her own.'

-o-

Olly the wise young tawny owl sat on his branch as dusk sneaked in around him. On his own as always, he let out the occasional 'Hoohoo' just to let his friends know he was still there, and still . . . alive. They never either replied or dropped by for a chat, which used to upset Olly . . . but not any more.

His grandpappy would always say that he would have to get used to being a solitary creature, because that's what tawny owls . . . were. Still, he couldn't help feeling lonely, no matter what other owls might say. If this was true, why was it he often heard other owls 'ke-witting' or 'hoohooing'? And occasionally he would see the odd couple or so swooping by on silent wings. How did they *do* that? Why was it that *he* had never been able to manage that?

His father had told him on several occasions that the ability to hunt for his food would come to him naturally, but he was never keen on killing these little creatures that all owls were supposed to enjoy. He knew that if he didn't do it, he could easily not survive. It wasn't too bad when he came upon a dead creature not far from his perch that he could eat, but occasionally it made him feel sick because sometimes the corpse he had discovered tasted like it had been there for a long time.

'Hoohoo!' he called this particularly dark and spooky night in the forest. 'For goodness' sake! It's pointless making such a racket when no one else is going to reply!'

'Mr Owl!' A foxy voice came up at him from the ground below. 'Olly? Are you there? Are you all right?'

'Who's that?' Olly replied cautiously, after a slight hesitation. 'And how do you know my *name*?'

'My name's Poppy, and I'm the fox that lives below you,' the young vixen answered almost in a whisper. 'Though you don't perch much higher than the bush I live under.'

'What do you mean?' the young owl answered. 'I live on a large branch just—'

'A very young tree sapling's height above the top of the bush I live under?' Poppy remarked. 'Why do you spend all of your time on a branch that is so close to the ground?'

'Well, if we're asking personal questions, why do you never leave your hollow under that dense mass of brambles?' Olly said sharply.

Silence descended, blotting out all sound around this unlikely pair.

'I don't like the dark!' Poppy replied quickly.

'I can't get on with heights!' Olly added almost at the same time.

'How do you survive when you can't hunt for your food?' the owl asked. 'Surely . . . ?'

'I couldn't manage without family,' Poppy explained. 'You?'

'Similarly here,' Olly added. 'And I find the occasional dead body a little . . .'

'Yew! Yuk!' the young fox said, almost throwing up at the thought.

'I don't have many – or even *any* – friends that call to be . . . friendly, either,' Olly admitted timidly.

'No friends?' Poppy gasped, seemingly shocked at what she was hearing. 'Actually, neither have I. The ones I used to have couldn't handle how I was, and didn't even want to *try* to understand.'

'You seem to have so much in common with each other,' a lighter and friendlier voice said. 'Why don't you become friends?'

They were so surprised to hear some other creature saying what they needed to hear that they both turned round sharply, Olly nearly falling from his very low perch and Poppy almost catching her luscious reddy-brown coat on overhanging brambles.

'Don't do that!' Olly gasped in shock.

'Who do you think you are?' Poppy shouted at almost the same time.

'My name is Patty,' the butterfly responded. 'I couldn't help but hear how sad you sounded.'

'And what is that to you?' Olly asked sharply.

'Nobody should be alone in this world when there are *so* many people who *are*,' Patty suggested. 'Such a lot of folks desperately want to have friends and family, to be loved and looked after, that being alone should not be an option. You two, for example, are beginning to understand each other, and although you are both from different families and backgrounds, you seem to be finding the common ground that such friends need.'

Poppy the sharp red fox and Olly the wise young tawny owl looked at each other and started to nod in agreement. They had been so caught up with their own individual problems that they had never thought about what Patty had seen straight away.

'She's right, you know,' Poppy agreed. 'Do you think we might be . . . you know—?'

'Friends?' Olly butted in. 'We're not natural family but we could perhaps become—'

'Natural friends?' Poppy added, a smile beginning to grow across her hairy face.

'Indeed, yes,' Olly agreed. 'Why can't an owl and a fox become the best of friends? I'm game – if you'll pardon the pun. How about you, my good friend Poppy?'

'Deal!' she said with a chuckle. 'Pleased to meet you, dear Olly.'

She held her front paw up towards her new friend, inviting a high five – or high four, as it turned out – which made them both feel good.

'You are so right, Patty Butterfly,' Olly said as they both turned round to thank her.

Once again, she wasn't there. Did she *need* to be there now that the two different characters had found each other?

Year 4

Year 4 – Class of 2021/22

Marli L    Poppy S    Ethan H    Lewis A

Lily C    Nathan S    Ashton FWM    Arlo V

Ava S    Ruth B    Isobel M    Oliver J

Aubree-Belle C    Elliot R    William T    Phoebie N

Charlie-Lee P	 Elodie G	 Eliza F	 Daisy B
 Luethus B	 Tyler S	 Halle-Mai Y	 Linda J
 John-Connor D	 Kian S	 Riley R	 Eli M-W

Mrs Wood	 Mr Bester

Signatures

Riley

Adam

John Grey   Lily   Aubree
Nathan
                                    Linola
Amelia   Ava   Marli   Kian   Poppy

              Lewis   Isobel
Lucthus   Phoebe   Daisy   Tyler
                        Elliot
                                        Elodie
         Eliza
              Charlie-Lee   Hollie-rain

Ethan   Eli   Ruth

                Liam

Chapter 6

October was never a good time to live near Old Man River, as the autumn rains seemed to go on forever and floods were inevitable. The only beneficiaries of this were waterfowl, other aquatic creatures, and fishermen. Most feathered fisher-folk like egrets, herons and other waders definitely missed out, because in flood waters their legs were too short to fulfil their normal function and food, then, was in short supply.

Pinky the flamingo often wished that she had been born a duck.

'No! No!' she muttered to herself as she stared into the rising water and shuffled uncomfortably about in the reeds close to the riverbank where she preferred to be. 'I don't like this one little bit!'

She dipped her toes gently into the chilly waters to make her final decision as to whether she should follow her instinct to wade and look for breakfast, deciding finally that this was not for her. Now, where to go for her first meal of the day? Or was it her first meal of the *week*?

She had actually taken a couple of floating, dead, glassy-eyed fish from close to the riverbank – which had almost made her sick –

along with a few green plants that her mother had always told her were good for the digestion, but nothing that *should* sustain her. She needed those pink wriggly creatures that would not only make her feel full and well but would also give her that pinky sheen to her feathers. They could only be found in Flamingo Wading Water, which did not run so fast. Was she searching in the correct place?

'I . . . don't . . . know! Where should I go? What should I do?' she mumbled, not really expecting an answer to float along that fast-flowing river to her.

'Good gracious!' A deep gravelly voice interrupted Pinky's conversation with herself.

She lifted her huge turned-under beak on her long slender neck to see an incredibly colourful butterfly sitting on the back of a tortoise's carapace.

'Am I very much mistaken, or is that a—?' Mabel the tortoise observed.

'An almost pink flamingo?' Patty the gloriously patterned butterfly replied.

'I thought flamingos were supposed to be all-over pink?' Mabel commented, a very puzzled look tormenting her face.

'They are,' her companion rider agreed. 'I think it all depends on diet.'

'Diet?' Mabel queried. 'What does *that* mean?'

'What they eat by dipping their head into the water,' Patty

said. 'Supposed to be little shrimpy creatures and some planty things.'

'Just a minute!' Pinky the flamingo bubbled. 'Are you talking about me? About me?'

'We were wondering why you aren't in the water looking for something to eat,' Patty asked.

'I don't like water because it's too deep, too fast, and I can't . . . swim,' Pinky tried to explain. 'Can't swim, although not sure what that is.'

'Does that mean, then, that you don't eat the things you *should* . . . eat?' Mabel asked. 'I've got to say that you do look as if you need a good square meal.'

'My beak and throat are too small to eat anything . . . square, I'm sure,' Pinky said, not really understanding what Mabel was trying to say. 'My mother tried to explain some time ago that I need to live where other creatures like me live, but I don't know where that might be.

'If I *did* find a place like that, wouldn't they eat *all* the food before I could get there?' Pinky went on, after a short pause for thought.

'It would mean that you might have to get there and stay to be able to feed properly,' Patty advised the unsure flamingo.

'How would I find such a place, and wouldn't it be too far to walk?' Pinky asked, with her obviously confused and dizzy reasoning.

'You have some things that I wish *I* had,' Mabel said. 'And they are called . . . wings.'

'What are they supposed to do?' the flamingo asked, a seriously puzzled look crowding her tiny flamingo eyes.

'They allow you to take off and . . . fly,' Patty explained. 'Watch me.'

Without fuss, the butterfly lifted off from Mabel's shell and fluttered around her companions to show how easy it was. Pinky would, of course, because of her size, need quite a lot of practice and space, but Patty and Mabel had her wellbeing in their minds. Whatever it was going to take, they would be there to help.

As the butterfly came in to land, she shouted, 'Look up there, Pinky. What do you see?'

The flamingo jerked her head upwards to catch two of her type in low flight over the river, with wings almost level and still, as they came in to land over the nearby woods, before disappearing from sight.

'Where are they going? What is over those tall things?' Pinky asked almost excitedly. 'Where—?'

'Over those trees you will find a shallow lake that doesn't flow at all,' Patty explained, slowly enough for her to understand. 'It is shallow enough for you to wade through the water to be with flamingos like you. You will find, however, that they are much pinker than you are.'

'Why should that be?' the flamingo bubbled excitedly. 'Aren't we all the same?'

'Indeed you are, but the difference is that they eat small creatures and plants that feed them properly, and help to colour their feathers pink,' Patty explained. 'Just a short flap of your wings away. How does that sound?'

'Exciting! Exciting!' Pinky gushed as she danced and jumped about, flapping her wings. Little did she realise that those flappy little feathered things were taking her higher and higher off the ground, before she landed again.

'Again! Again!' Mabel encouraged her. 'You're flying! You're flying!'

The last thing the two friends saw as Pinky took off and headed towards Flamingo Wading Water was a look of shock and delight rolled into one in her eyes.

'Thank you!' her voice floated down to her new friends. 'You are my bestest friends! I'll see you . . . '

Then she disappeared behind the trees, to be followed by several other, pinkier, flamingos on their way to their joint feeding place.

'Well, I never thought we'd give help to a creature like that one!' Mabel sighed. 'She is—'

'A lovely creature, as are all the "friends" we've met on our travels,' Patty said happily. 'That's what friends are for, don't you think?'

Chapter 7

'Mammy?' Dotty the little penguin asked her mother in that drawled-out whining sort of a way that *all* youngsters use when they want something or have an impossible question they want answering.

'Yes, Dotty?' Mammy replied with a sigh, almost reluctant to hear yet another question that was unnecessary to her but important to her daughter. 'What is it you need to know this time?'

'Why do we have to live where it's always very cold – almost too cold to live?' the youngster asked, just as her mammy had forecast. A serious question to which it was impossible to offer an answer.

'Well, my little one, this is where we have always lived, as far back as I, your grandparents and your great-grandpappy Isaac can remember,' Dotty's mammy explained, without providing the answer that Dotty wanted or needed.

'But—' Dotty began again, not really satisfied with her answer.

'Enough now, Dotty,' Mammy insisted. 'We don't ask those sorts of questions, because there is no real answer. We accept that we have always been here, and here is where we will always stay. Isn't that your friend, Dolly, over by the flat rocks, waving at you? Go along and play while I catch us our dinner, there's a pretty penguin.'

'All right, Mammy,' Dotty agreed. 'What's for dinner today?'

'Fish, I think,' her mother replied.

'Ooh, lovely!' Dotty said, excitedly punching the air with her curled flipper. 'My favourite!'

'Hello, Dolly,' Dotty gurgled as she swam over to her friend. 'Fancy swimming to Icy Island in the bay? We could practise diving off the hill at its side and—'

'Dolly!' her friend's name floated over from a group of penguins scything through the waves. 'Come on Dolly, time to catch dinner!'

'But—' Dotty muttered as her so-called friend darted off to meet her mother, leaving Dotty alone with no one else to play with. This wasn't what she wanted to happen. She turned round and headed slowly towards the pebbly beach around the ice floes nearby. Surely her friend Dolly ought to have come with her to play. *She* would have gone with Dolly! It was always the same. Dolly only came to play with Dotty when she had nothing better to do. They *did* have fun usually, though, when they swam around dodging the ice floes and leaping over the older penguins as they headed out to do their fishing and freedom feeding.

However, when Dolly found something more exciting to do with her 'other' friends, she always shot away, leaving Dotty on her own . . . *again*.

Mammy suggested she might be as well finding some new friends who might be more loyal to her, as friends should be, but Dotty always found it difficult to make new friends. Was this basically because she was a loner – someone who never attracted anyone to be her friend and to be friendly and loyal?

Having stopped swimming and floated on her back for a time to relax and cast the disappointments of the day out of her mind, she awoke with a start from a deep sleep. Not knowing where she was, she leapt to her stubby feet in panic, realising that the last time she was conscious, she was swimming around sadly, whereas now she found herself on a small ice floe that seemed to be melting slowly.

'No! No!' she gabbled in desperation. Dusk had closed in and was heading towards nightfall, making her realise that she was now adrift on her meagre little ice raft in the middle of a deserted ocean, not knowing which way was home. 'Oh no! My fish dinner! And I have no way of knowing which way to swim to get it, particularly in this darkness.'

As this little chinstrap penguin was too young to manage without her mammy, she thought it best to remain afloat in relative safety until daylight could point her in the right direction. There was no way she was about to attempt to swim in the forlorn hope she might find the right way, particularly with the dangers that could trap such a small creature on her own. She had been told about sharks and orcas – whatever *they* were – but had never seen one.

Perhaps what she had been told were just stories to frighten her, to make her take greater care in the ocean, and maybe those creatures were friendly and helpful. Perhaps even—

A gentle and softly spoken voice joined Dotty on her ice platform. 'Well, I don't think I have ever seen such a young chin-strap penguin on its own at this time of day before,' it said.

'You may well be alone on this unfriendly sea, but I wouldn't even try to make friends with sharks and orcas,' a much gruffer voice spoke up.

'Who are you and what are you doing—?' the little penguin asked, puzzled to see a small wooden boat tied up to the ice floe.

'In our boat fastened to your ice raft?' Mabel the tortoise said as she skidded on its surface, finding it very hard to keep her footing. 'I am a tortoise called Mabel, and my passenger is—'

'A rather chilly butterfly called Patty,' the butterfly butted in cheerily, despite the cold. 'We butterflies don't manage very well when it's as cold as this.'

'Then why are you here?' Dotty asked, unable to understand the thinking behind their appearance.

'We thought you might like a little company, although my friend here is anything but little,' Patty said with a smile. 'We wouldn't like you to feel alone.'

'We know you have only one friend, but she never behaves how a friend should behave,' Mabel said as she started to dig into the ice and snow.

'Why are you doing that?' Dotty asked the tortoise as *she* started to help, not really knowing why.

'I'm making a shelter so we can keep warmer,' Mabel replied.

'In snow and ice?' the penguin queried. 'Surely that would have the opposite effect, wouldn't it?'

'You will be surprised,' Mabel responded. 'Just about done. Coming into my makeshift shelter?'

'You've nothing to lose, and besides, it would not be a good idea to swim in the dark where there are creatures out there that can see *you* when *you* can't even hear *them*,' Patty explained. 'We're here to encourage you to do what you need to do . . . when it's light enough.'

'No chance!' Dotty said adamantly. 'I'll wait until we float closer to somewhere I recognise.

'You know, you're right,' the little penguin said after a while in silence. 'It *is* warmer in this little shelter. In fact, if I stay in here much longer, I will be *too* warm.'

-o-

Dawn broke slowly with no real excitement for the start of a new day . . . and with very little daylight or hope of having a lovely mouthful of fish for breakfast. As she believed her new companions were still asleep in their warm shelter, Dotty decided she might just slide quietly out of the shelter to hunt for something to eat.

Tobogganing along the ice on her belly so as not to make any noise, she reached the little ice raft's edge and plunged into the icy water, which woke her up very quickly. With a gasp and a paddle, she shot off to the depths to explore. She was as sure as a young chinstrap could be that a feast awaited her under the surface.

Surveying the scene behind her before she came up for air, she was surprised to see the frighteningly large shape of a black and white fish swimming at speed towards her with a smile on its face and its mouth wide open.

Convinced that *this* monster didn't have any good wishes for her, she put on as much speed as she was able to muster to escape from a grisly end in this creature's throat. Just as the pursuer was about to close its teeth around our little chinstrap penguin, she pressed the accelerator pedal and breached the ocean's surface in an almightily spectacular leap out of reach of this particular orca as its jaws snapped shut on . . . empty air.

She landed on the little ice raft with a resounding *plop!* and was only stopped from sliding off the opposite edge by Mabel's sturdy carapace. No doubt those same massive jaws would have been waiting, wide open, at the other side of the ice floe had Mabel not applied the brakes pretty stoutly.

'Well now,' Patty said gravely. 'Not a very successful swim?'

'No fish to fill your belly?' Mabel suggested.

'Fortunately, I can see the penguin I believe to be your mammy on the ice not a million flipper flaps from here,' Patty said, pointing an antenna towards a worried-looking group of older chinstrap penguins and one or two youngsters who desperately wanted to hear about Dotty's adventure. 'You see, our floe has floated back to land from where you started yesterday, I believe.'

'I can't thank you enough, Patty and Mabel, for saving me and—' Dotty said as she turned towards her new friends, to see their little boat sailing away into a gloriously sunny day.

'Another success, perhaps?' Mabel muttered to her companion as a gathering breeze took to the sail they had raised.

'I do believe you may be right,' Patty answered. 'Spectacular leap from that dear little chinstrap, though, don't you think?'

Year 5

Year 5 – Class of 2021/22

Poppy P

Daisy P

Alfie Y

Joshua H K

Luke R

Leo C

Reilly C

Alfie T

Lacie S

Lilly S

Euan B

Annie-Jane B

Jake H

Kane K

William P

Louis K

Sophia D	Logan K	Lexi-Mai F	Nina S
Oscar P	George B	Ava-Rose P	Ella B
Evie B	Ruby H	Charlie A	Alisha E
Alfie H	Miss Lee	Ms Mullineux	Miss Lund

Signatures

Ruby Kaneg Luke

George lacie
Oliver leo

Alfie Nina Sophia

Lilly Daisy Louis logan
Ella W.P

Jake Ava-Rose Anie

Abbie H charlie
Alisha

Joshua Ellen Poppy Leah-mai

Chapter 8

Mabel the young tortoise couldn't believe how amazing this day had been. Gloriously warm sunshine had heated up her cold-blooded body enough for her almost to grow a tan on her pale carapace.

Since she had wandered out into the clear, warm morning, she had felt happier than she had ever felt before. The amount of delicious dandelion leaves and luscious yellow flowers she had consumed the day before had made sure she would sleep like the proverbial log.

Unfortunately, this didn't happen quite as well as she had hoped.

Snuggling down in the warm family burrow with Mama and Papa and her three brothers and two sisters was no problem once they had *all* decided that snuggling was what they needed to do. The difficulty, of course, lay in her brothers' desire to carry on playing when everyone else needed to snooze. They were excited that the next day was home removal day, when they were to take all their worldly belongings (which were mostly straw and food) to a much bigger and more comfortable dwelling closer to the oak forest, where an inexhaustible food source neighboured their new home. How wonderful that was going to be!

Once her brothers and sisters had been overtaken by the desire to snooze away the rest of the night, their immediate drop into deep, silent sleep lasted just . . . ten minutes. This lulled Mabel into a false drift into what was promising to be a lovely, warm, cosy and enjoyably deep slumber.

The sighing sound from each young tortoise developed slowly, and drifted alarmingly into a rasping, rumbling bout of incessant . . . snoring, which was made worse by its resonating in the carapace each bore. Incessantly, boringly loud and very *disturbing* . . . snoring!

'Mabel!' Mama's quiet voice broke into her slumbering dreams once she had finally fallen into that wonderful well of exciting adventures. 'Time to get up. It won't be long before we are away to our new home. Breakfast's on the table. Quickly now.'

'Wha . . . What . . . ?' she mumbled, unable to believe it was that time already. 'But I haven't been asleep yet because of all their snoring. A few more moments, Mama, please?'

'If you don't come now, your breakfast will be in your brothers' and sisters' stomachs,' Mama replied. 'Your choice.'

When she stumbled into the eating room, rubbing sleep from her still-tired eyes, she noticed that she was . . . alone.

'Mama! Pappa!' she called as she nibbled on her breakfast. 'Are you there? Mama!'

Walking slowly outside, the bottom of her shell stuffed with tasty morsels she hadn't had time to consume, she was astounded to see that she *was* completely alone.

'What am I going to do with all this food?' she muttered to herself, not quite sure where everyone else had gone. 'I know! I'll eat it. All of it.'

Having eaten a whole day's rations, she plumped her body into a shallow hollow filled with comfortable, fresh grass, now feeling not only the pressure of a very full belly, but also her lack of sleep from the night before. Sleep very quickly kidnapped her, thrusting her into a black void from which there was no immediate escape.

'I think I know where they've gone!' she shouted, waking up startlingly quickly for a tortoise. 'The new burrow!'

Unfortunately, she had never paid much attention to any of the conversations her parents had had about their new abode, and so she had only a vague idea where it might be.

'Sitting here just won't do,' she mumbled as she heaved herself with difficulty out of the comfortable hollow. 'Which way first, eh?'

As she lifted one of her front legs to put her best foot forward, she felt something tickling her nose so violently, it made her cross her eyes.

'Wha . . . ?' she gasped, feeling she was being attacked by an invisible invader. 'What on earth's going on?'

Because of the creature she was, she was unable to waft away whatever it was that was bothering her. So she began to withdraw her neck and head into her carapace to try to remove the thing that tickled her face mercilessly.

'Thank goodness for that.' Mabel sighed with relief as whatever had irritated her face had stopped once her neck was fully withdrawn into her shell.

'Why did you do that?' a light yet attractive voice asked a few moments later.

'Who said that?' Mabel muttered, almost indistinguishably.

'I'm sorry, I can't make out what you are saying,' the newcomer replied. 'Can you come out and speak more clearly, please?'

'I said . . . goodness gracious me!' the tortoise gasped, aghast at what she saw sitting before her on a stout grass stalk. 'You're a—'

'Butterfly?' the gloriously coloured creature answered.

'I once knew a butterfly called Patty,' Mabel said, a bit of a distant look in her eyes. 'We were friends for ages, it seemed. We tortoises can live for a very long time, you see, but butterflies . . . can't.'

'I'm called Patty Two,' the butterfly said.

'Patty as well, eh?' the tortoise asked.

'No. Patty *number* two,' the butterfly explained quite simply. 'You see, all female butterflies of our sort are born with the name Patty. I am the second one with that name, hence Patty Two. I know what kindnesses you two did for many other creatures, and as she is now elsewhere in our wonderful world, I was wondering if we might be friends to carry on where you and she left off?'

'I don't see why not,' Mabel agreed. 'It would be fun to help other youngsters similarly. We can probably start with . . . me.'

'You've lost both your parents, brothers and sisters, and your way, I feel,' Patty Two suggested. 'Would you like help to find them?'

'Just so I know where to find them when *we* are between projects,' Mabel assured her.

-o-

'Oh dear! Oh dear!' Red the little fox cub muttered, afraid of what was going to happen next. He had been separated from his mother for just over a day, obliging him to spend his first frightening night alone.

He didn't like this! He didn't like it at all!

He stumbled around the large clearing in these fearful woods, surrounded by a frightening wall of tree boles/trunks that refused to allow him to be released. Every time he came across the slightest gap between the trees, the clearing seemed to close it when Red approached. It was most frustrating and more than a little disturbingly frightening.

Difficult questions that needed answers crowded his terrified mind. Why had his mother not found him by now? Had she meant to leave him to fend for himself? If so, why? Would he be able to find her? Did she *want* to be found?

Although he couldn't find a way out and he was very worried that he would stay in this clearing for the rest of his life, the golden sunbeams slanted down from above, lighting the inside of the tree wall and the hard soil floor beneath his feet. He was beginning to panic, because he could see no way out.

'Hello.' A kind-sounding soft voice interrupted Red's panic. 'Are you all right?'

The appearance of this new voice startled Red the fox cub and set him back on his haunches, fear causing his eyes to widen and stare at the newcomers.

'What . . . ? Who . . . ? How . . . ?' he stammered when confronted by them.

'My name is Mabel,' the tortoise replied.

'And I'm Patty Two,' her companion added.

'But how—?' Red gabbled, perplexed by their appearance.

'Did we get here?' Mabel continued.

'When *you* can't find your way out?' Patty Two said, her soft, kind voice having a seriously calming effect on the cub's raw fear. His eyes were still fearful of these two strangers whose magical appearance disturbed him, but they were not now quite as wide and unblinking as before.

'We could see that you were having . . . difficulties,' Patty Two explained. 'As we were just passing through this lovely forest, we felt we had to drop in and say hello, trying to offer assistance in your time of need.'

'Thank you,' the fox cub said in his quiet little voice that was almost a whisper. 'I have lost my way and can't find my mama.'

'I would imagine that your mother will be searching for you frantically,' Patty Two assured him. 'Don't give up – we are here to help you find your way out of these fabulously friendly trees. Would you like to come along with us, and we'll find a way out?'

'I don't think I had better—' Red replied reluctantly.

'Come with two strangers to find your way home?' Mabel offered. 'We understand that your mother has probably warned you about that sort of thing quite a while ago, and we agree.'

'Tell you what,' Patty Two suggested. 'How about if Mabel stays here and you follow me to that gap between those slender sapling sycamore trees over to your right? Then with a couple of beats of your beautiful brush we may well find what you have been looking for. Agreed?'

'Er . . . yes, I suppose so,' Red replied, a little more bravely and with far less of a startled, frightened look resting in his eyes.

'Come on, then!' Patty Two called back as she took off gracefully, dancing along the gentle airs in front of her charge. The much braver little reddy-brown fox trotted behind her, gaining in confidence as they moved along.

Approaching the trees once again, there remained a little apprehension in his mind until the trees disappeared abruptly and unexpectedly.

'There he is!' one of his brothers shouted loudly, forcing his mother to turn around sharply, a look of profound relief in her face as she grasped her missing son and drew him to her.

'Where have you been, and how did you just appear like that?' Mama Fox said with a heartfelt sigh, glad to have her son back in the pack.

'I became lost two days ago, and two kind and friendly folks found me and brought me back here,' Red started his story. 'One of them here is a butterfly called Patty Two, and her friend, Mabel, is a tortoise who is in those trees over there.'

He turned around to introduce his saviours to his pack, to find that not only were they not there, but neither was the clearing of trees.

Although Red was confused and puzzled in equal amounts, he was also extremely glad to be back with his family, all of whom had drawn him into their close circle once again.

chapter 9

'So this is the River Sticks?' Mabel said to Patty Two as they settled for a rest to watch its clear waters drifting lazily towards an unknown end. 'Time for a bit of a rest and a snooze, perhaps?'

'Well, a bit of a rest, anyway,' Patty Two agreed.

'Could you just explain to me a couple of concerns?' Mabel asked, having settled down in a soft and comfortable hollow under the eaves of a small wood by the river's bank, for a rest.

'Of course I can,' Patty Two replied confidently. 'Since when have you known me not be able to do that?'

'All right,' Mabel responded, her brow creased in concentration. 'As we've been walking for quite some time – and I use the word 'we' advisedly – isn't it time we had a rest and a modicum of . . . refreshment? I'm starving, and I glimpsed a rather attractive clump of dandelions – in full flower, I hasten to add – that might provide us with a degree of sustenance.'

'Don't like dandelions, as I thought you knew,' Patty Two said, to her friend's surprise.

'Don't like . . . ?' Mabel gasped, almost unable to believe that there was anyone in the known universe that didn't like . . . 'I thought everybody—'

'Everybody but *me*,' Patty Two butted in. 'However, in my travels I have seen both dandelions and – my favourite – white and pink clover together in the same wildflower field.'

'Come on, then,' Mabel sighed. 'Where is this bountiful supply of the most wonderful sunshine food available to us? Over the river, I suppose?'

'Well, er, in a word . . . yes,' Patty Two replied quietly.

'I'm afraid I never got round to learning how to swim when I was a youngster,' Mabel said, more than a little sarcastically. 'And I don't see any boatmen available to give me a lift. *You* could always flit across and bring me a morsel or two back while I sit and have a snooze or two right here.

'That was a joke!' Mabel continued, after a moment's silence from her friend. 'No sense of humour, some folk.'

Without any further comment, Patty Two took off and flitted in that crazy up-and-down kind of flight she always used, and disappeared around the next turn the river took.

Knowing that Patty Two would be away for a while, Mabel settled down in her cosy and comfortable bower, and was asleep very quickly.

-o-

Having been asleep for only a very brief time, Mabel awoke to an annoying tickling feeling on her snout. Blowing through her nostrils to try to rid herself of this infuriating sensation, she opened her eyes one at a time. All she could see was a vibrant blaze of colour cutting out all other sights.

A very familiar voice drifted to the tortoise's ears. 'Are you all right, Mabel?'

'Who's that?' the tortoise replied, still seemingly confused. 'Is that you, Mother?'

'No, silly. It's me,' Patty Two assured her friend.

'Only joking,' Mabel giggled mischievously. 'I knew it was you. You've not been gone long. Been somewhere interesting and exciting?'

'Round the bend—' Patty Two started to explain, to be interrupted sharply by her friend.

'I always thought there was something not quite right about you.' Mabel sniggered again.

'There is a ferryman . . . by a boat . . . offering to give folks a ride across the River Sticks,' Patty Two explained, ignoring her friend's attempts at being funny. This was probably because butterflies were never considered to have any sense of humour. 'He is a very dark-coloured fox who may even have a touch of wolf in him. He is called Blackie, and he says he is Red's brother. You remember Red?'

'Of course I do!' Mabel insisted loudly. 'He was the little red fox that became trapped in the circle of trees, and . . . in his own mind.'

'That's the one,' Patty Two agreed. 'Well? If you have a ride in his little ferry boat, we'll be across the River Sticks in no time, ready for our dinner.'

'You *do* realise that it will take me quite a while to get to him,' Mabel pointed out. 'Will he still be there tomorrow?'

'How often have we done without our dinner?' Patty Two asked. 'He'll still be there, have no fear. Besides, it's only just round that small copse of trees by the riverbank.'

Pointing out where they were heading, she lifted off and, in her disjointed way of flying, she fluttered back and forth, encouraging Mabel to keep pace. The path ahead was clear and flat, allowing the tortoise to make good time. They had all the time in the world, and the ferryman didn't seem to be going anywhere soon.

'Well, well,' a gruff, wheedling sort of a voice accosted them as they approached the river. 'What sort of an odd-looking creature have we here? Blackie the Ferryman at your service, good people. Anyone for a trip across this glorious river, or perhaps even a short cruise to see the sights, or even' – he dropped to a secretive whisper, looking over both shoulders to see that no one else was listening – 'across to the farmer's field to check out his field of cabbages? Your choice of one, two or all three.'

'I don't eat cabbages, and I wouldn't thank you for a lengthy cruise up and down this boring river,' Mabel snorted, gruffly and honestly. 'So a crossing, as sharp as you can make it, would be my choice.'

'All right. I'll get the boat ready,' Blackie said, inching away.

'He's not a ferryman,' Patty Two whispered quietly once the wolf had sloped off to the boat.

'Not a . . . ?' her friend whispered back, equally quietly. 'How do you know?'

'Notice the pointy end of the boat?' Patty Two replied. 'There is no way that will make it even a boat length in this water. It has a rather large hole in it, *and* it doesn't look as if it has been moved from this point for a very long time.'

'What do you think he's up to, then?' Mabel gasped.

'He's up to no good,' Patty Two added. 'So we had better watch him closely.'

'All ready, then,' Blackie said with a chuckle, rubbing his paws together. 'Into the boat, if you please, ready for your crossing to the . . . other side.'

As the wolf started to push the boat a little further into the river, a rogue current jerked its bow out of his paws, causing him to crack a hind leg on an invisible rock. Losing his balance, he catapulted forward, banging his head on the rear of the boat as it swung around, out of control. Very rapidly, it filled with water and disappeared into the depths.

'Help!' Blackie yelped. 'Help! I can't swim!'

As the tip of his very thin tail flashed past the tortoise, she snapped at it and caught its tender tip in her sharp beak.

'Arghh!' he yelped, in pain. 'Please! Arghh!'

Impervious to his anguished cries, Mabel dragged his unresisting body back to land, where she dropped him in a very gooey heap of . . . sticky, clayey mud, with her bony beak still grasping his tail for dear life.

'And your intentions weren't entirely honest and honourable, were they?' Patty Two remonstrated with the half-breed.

'No! Arghh! I don't know!' he yelled again, in considerable discomfort.

'Don't forget, my friend, that Mabel will not let go until you tell the truth,' Patty Two continued. 'Hm? Well?'

'All right! All right!' Blackie pleaded urgently as his throbbing tail tip made him increasingly aware of his nasty, tricksy mind. 'I apologise for my unpleasantness.'

'Should I let him go, Patty Two?' Mabel asked her friend. 'Or should I squeeze more—?'

'No! No! Please?' the foxy wolf pleaded again.

'Have you never had family or friends to look up to before?' Mabel said, once she had loosened her tight grip on his tail.

'No, not really,' Blackie whimpered, sitting hunched on his haunches, trying to soothe his tail tip. 'Pappa fell into a mountain ravine when I was a cub, and Mama couldn't cope with me and my five brothers. So we were left to our own devices, scuffing scraps to eat, scrabbling about without anywhere real to call home, and making ends meet wherever we could. That is when I learnt to be devious and dreadfully badly behaved.'

'Wow! What a shame,' Mabel said, understanding the poor way he had been brought up and how he hadn't been set a good example of appropriate behaviour.

'We will, of course, be around for quite some time, to help wherever and however we can,' Patty Two offered. 'But only if you feel you would like to change.'

'I can see how important it must be to be friendly and helpful to others,' Blackie returned. 'So, please, I would be grateful for your help.'

'By the way, you don't know of anyone who might have a boat to take me across the river to the fabulous field of food, do you?' Mabel asked, more in hope than in certainty.

'No need,' he said, standing up on all fours while wagging his – now painless – wolfy tail. 'Follow me, because round the next bend there is a little wooden footbridge across the very much narrower part of the river. I'll show you the way.'

Chapter 10

'Why do we have to live in a country with such a ridiculously cold climate?' Mabel the tortoise muttered as she squeezed out of the comfortably warm little shelter that she called home. She only had to extend her concertina neck just past the doorway to experience an icy breeze that wanted to wrap itself round the *portable* home she called a carapace.

'*You* think this is cold and inclement!' Patty Two the beautiful butterfly gasped. 'How do you think *I* feel? Don't forget I can't cope even for a few minutes in this cold and survive. I think it's going to be too cold to venture out today.'

'All right,' Mabel answered. 'I'll bring you something to sustain you. Any preference?'

'I'll leave it to you, my friend,' Patty Two assured her. 'You might even find me on the verge of hibernation when you return.'

She found it difficult to move quickly at the best of times, and these icy conditions made matters very much worse, allowing her only to stutter and stumble forward. However, not one to give up easily, Mabel set off in her slow and jerky way, with her head perched precariously on her extended neck so she might see clearly where she was heading.

The time Mabel and Patty Two had spent with Blackie the foxy wolf still preyed on her mind, making her wonder whether they did the right thing when they left him to his own devices. They both thought they had spent enough time in his company, showing him how creatures needed to be kind and supportive of each other. They *hoped* he would have learnt, but you never could be too certain.

'Hello,' a gruffly rasping voice accosted Mabel's ears as she shuffled through a thicket of evergreen shrubs on her slow way to find some sustenance for her friend. 'You're a tortoise, aren't you?'

Mabel's instant response was to draw her neck and head into her shell very rapidly until she was able to assess any danger to her being.

'Don't be afraid,' the voice urged her, less loudly. 'Although some of my extended family love to *eat* tortoise, I don't – and besides, you are at least as big as me and probably many times harder.'

Looking carefully around, Mabel could see . . . nothing. Feeling that this voice might be an echo from some of the surrounding hills, she allowed her head to emerge from her shell very slowly.

'Hello again,' the gruff voice hailed, this time from just above her head. 'Don't you want to talk to me, Mr Tortoise?'

Mabel glanced upwards very carefully, to see an untidy and very hairy upside-down face just above hers.

'If you would like me to acknowledge that you even exist, you will have to come down to my level upside-up,' Mabel retorted, more than a little irked by this creature's intrusion. '*Who* are you, *what* are you, and what do you want?'

'I am Mellirocco, or Melli for short, or even Rocco if you prefer,' the creature replied, a puzzled look in his eyes but a trace of a smile gracing his mouth. 'I am a small bear.'

'And why do you need to speak to me?' the tortoise asked, not sure that she really needed an answer. 'I don't think we have anything in common. I am a tortoise who likes to eat dandelions, and you are a bear who likes to eat . . . tortoises? Good luck with that one, unless your teeth are made of granite!'

'I . . . do . . . not . . . eat . . . tortoises!' Rocco protested. 'Or any other creature – except for frogs and insects and . . . rodents, that is. My favourite food is honeybee larvae . . . oh, and . . . honey. *That* is my *best* food.'

At the mention of honey, his jaw began to quiver, and he started to dribble saliva from the of corners his mouth, as his tongue flapped around his open mouth. He sat down with a bump on a largish tuft of couch grass, which made his eyes jump and his teeth clamp shut.

'Can I take it, then, that you are here to ask for help and advice about where you might locate this . . . honey?' Mabel asked, slowly and non-committally. 'What makes you think a tortoise might know where this "honey" stuff might be found?'

'I don't really know,' Rocco answered after a few minutes, a disappointed look growing on his dishevelled hairy face. 'I just thought you might . . . know . . . and this is my last hope.'

'Just a minute,' Mabel uttered, stretching her neck out fully as she sniffed the air about them. 'Isn't that . . . *honey* I can smell on *you*?'

'Er, well, I think it might be,' Rocco answered reluctantly. 'What of it?'

'Did you never consider that it might be important?' Mabel said, pouncing on his omission. 'Or that I might be able to help because I can smell a bee's nest a thousand paces away?'

'I'm sorry,' Rocco said. 'It might just have slipped my . . . mind. You can *tell* where honey might be found? I'm a honey bear, and even *I* can't do that.

'I am desperate!' Rocco explained, after a moment of wringing his paws. 'You would be my friend for life.'

Once Mabel started to move away slowly, Rocco asked in panic, 'Where are you going? Please help me!'

'Follow me.' The tortoise threw the words over her shoulder without stopping to look where she was going. The very faint scent of a bees' hive drew her onwards with unerring accuracy, along paths not trodden before, through tree copses and dense bushes, to a small cave at the foot of a large hill overlooking a fast-moving and very winding river.

The entrance to the cave was almost obliterated by a dense cloud of individually moving bees – workers helping to construct a chamber for their queen, and gatherers bringing nectar to feed all and sundry.

'Is this what you wanted?' Mabel asked the little bear as she stopped at a safe and respectful distance from the swarm.

'Yes! Yes!' Rocco shouted, bumbling clumsily forward to tear apart the rough hive in his desperate quest for his favourite food.

'Stop! Stop!' Mabel yelled, gripping one of his hind paws as he tried to blunder past her.

'Ow! Ow! Ow!' he yelled, as he was stopped by a sharp pain to his leg. 'Let me go! Let me go!'

When he saw that the tortoise meant business, he dropped to the floor of the cave on all fours, with his forepaws covering his face.

'You . . . will . . . *not* . . . destroy the hive!' Mabel ordered him, once she had let go of his paw. 'We need to be very careful and gentle, otherwise the bees will disappear, and so will your dinner.'

She plumped her shell onto the floor and very quietly explained to Rocco how he was going to collect *some* honey. It was all that he could do to restrain himself from gathering all he could, once he had eaten his fill.

'There is one thing I want you to do as a repayment for all my help,' Mabel said, 'and that is to follow me back to my dwelling. It won't take long.'

-o-

'Patty Two!' Mabel called as they approached the cave. 'Patty Two! Please come out.'

After much complaining throughout their journey back, Rocco threw himself down onto the grass before the entrance to the cave, wanting both to go back to the bees' hive and to escape into the wild.

'What is it?' Patty Two asked, not understanding why Mabel had brought this rough-looking creature back to their cave. 'Why have you brought this . . . honey bear?'

'If you flutter over and settle on his face, you'll understand why,' the tortoise urged. 'No, don't be concerned. He won't hurt you. Go on.'

Patty Two flitted over and landed on the bear's nose.

'Well?' the tortoise asked. 'What do you smell or see?'

'Oh, my goodness!' Patty Two gasped. 'Honey! All for me?'

'Indeed,' her friend said. 'Go on! Take your fill. Our friend, Rocco, is more than happy to share.'

Year 6

Year 6 – Class of 2021/22

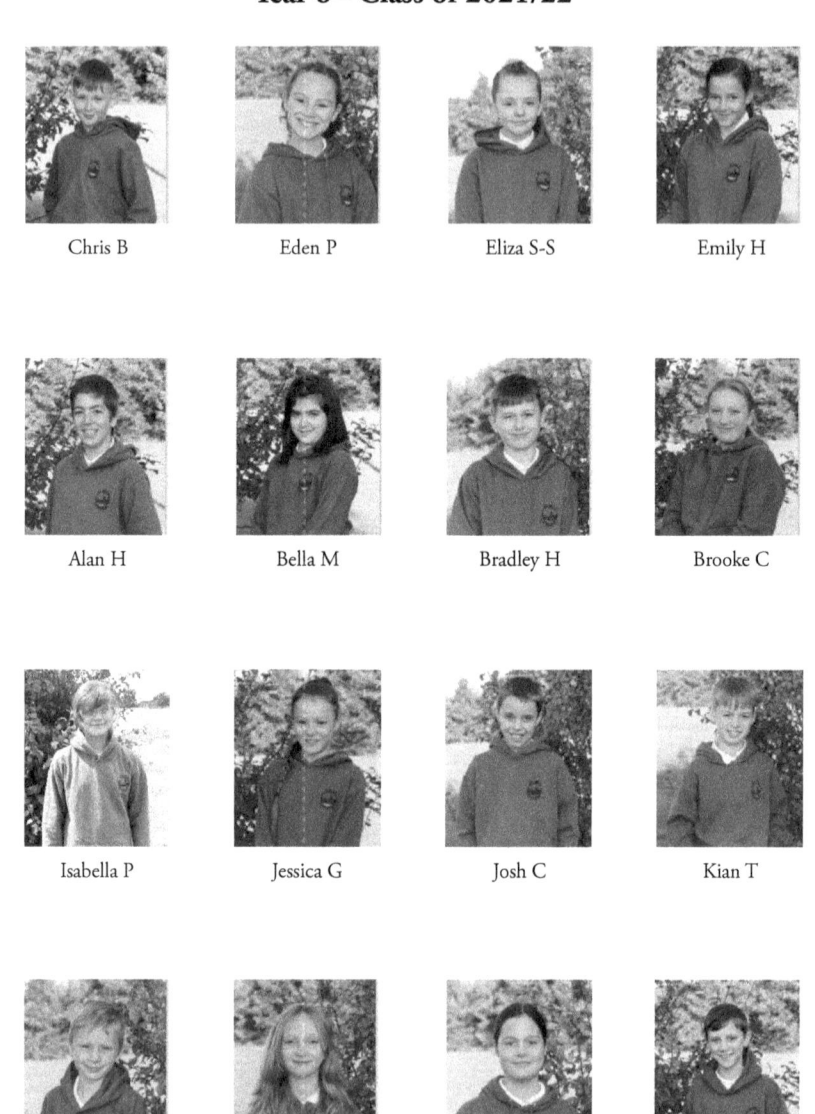

Chris B	Eden P	Eliza S-S	Emily H
Alan H	Bella M	Bradley H	Brooke C
Isabella P	Jessica G	Josh C	Kian T
George S	Georgia S	Gracie E	Jack R

Salvatore D	 Shalom B	 Vinnie H	 Willow D
 Lexi C-J	 Mason G	 Nancy S	 Noah S
 Oliver C	 Pearl P	 Penny R	 Rae M-G

Miss Garnett	 Leon K	 Mrs Pace

Signatures

Bella Rae   Penny

Bradley   Nancy

Josh   George
            Noah
Mason   Jack   Kian

Willow   Gracie   Chris

               Georgia   Oliver

Pearl   Brooke
        Eden   Salvatore   Emily

Vinnie   Jessica

        Leon
                           Shalom
Isabella   Eliza   Alan   Lexi

Chapter 11

'This is a fine mess you have gotten yourself into!' Isabella the fennec fox grumbled at herself as she tried to disengage her once-lovely fur from the dense and evil bramble bush. 'How on earth did you allow *this* to happen, you silly girl? I know you were minding your own business, causing nobody any harm, then whoosh! Brambles here we come!'

Isabella had never been a popular creature, ever since shortly after her birth, when her mother went out to hunt one day and never came back, leaving her with her father and six siblings. He, of course, spent much of *his* time hunting for food, spending time with his buddies, and . . . sleeping. He had no idea how to look after youngsters, feeding and nurturing them until they were able to do it for themselves.

Isabella never learnt how to do that, because she was the youngest by quite some way and saw her mother only twice at suckling before she disappeared. She was pushed around and mocked a lot by her siblings, causing her to sit on her haunches a lot during each day, sucking her paw for comfort and feeling very hungry. Her diet consisted mostly of the earthworms and beetles that stumbled accidentally into the family's den, which didn't allow her much of a balanced diet – when she had any diet at all.

Because she was never viewed as part of the family, her siblings never included her in any of their activities, for two main reasons. First, she was too young and weak to participate in their rough-and-tumbles, and second, she didn't look anything like any of them. They were pale and short-furred, and *she* looked more like a cross between a fox and a wolf cub, with a lush, deep, reddish-brown coat.

'Well, that's a first,' a deeply raspy sort of a voice accosted the little fox who was convinced she came from fennec ancestry. 'I've seen hairy creatures caught on low tree branches and in very dense hawthorn bushes before, but never reclining in the middle of a bramble bush. It seems like this one has just been dropped there.' As this tortoise was talking, a gloriously colourful butterfly alighted gently on its carapace, furled its wings and sat quietly in the dappled sunlight, seeming to listen to what the tortoise was saying.

'Would it be possible to give me a hand to extricate myself from these dreadful brambles, please?' the little fox pleaded, almost apologetically. 'You see, I don't remember very clearly as yet how I got . . . here, but it *is* beginning to come back to me . . . by degrees.'

'Of course we can,' the butterfly replied softly, nodding to her companion. 'My name's Patty Two, and my dear friend is called Mabel.'

'I'm Isabella and I am very pleased you came along when you did,' the little reddy-brown fox said, her eyes beginning to show a bit more life. 'I didn't feel like I would be able to go on much longer when . . . Whoops! Aargh!'

'There we are, little Isabella,' Mabel said with a giggle. 'You are now . . . free.'

'Oh, thank you, thank you, thank you,' Isabella gushed, shaking her fur to disengage the bramble thorns and sticky bits.

'What's the matter with your eye?' Patty Two asked, rather concerned that streaks of blood were dripping from the fox's eye corner. 'It's injured! Did the thorns cause that?'

'I don't . . . think so,' she replied slowly. 'I am now beginning to remember how things were at home with my brothers and sisters and . . . everything, I suppose, really.'

'Didn't you have any friends that could have supported you?' Mabel asked, feeling very sorry for the little creature.

'Mama suckled me twice only and then she went out and didn't return,' Isabella explained. 'I had three brothers and two sisters, as far as I can remember. They didn't like me, and my father was never at home, leaving just me . . . on my own.'

'You can count?' Mabel gasped. 'A tiny very young cub that can . . . count? That's amazing.'

'Yes, I can.' The little fox puffed out her chest, beginning to gain in confidence. 'I have one tail, four paws, two ears – except that I can only see the outside flaps – and two eyes, although one of them was damaged by a big . . . owl? There! I can remember *that* at least now.'

'Big owl?' Patty Two, who had been listening to the pathetic tale, butted in. 'I didn't know—'

'Been around for some time,' Mabel interrupted. 'Always picking up little stray creatures to carry away to eat. You wouldn't expect it to try it on with a fox, but *this* fox is *tiny*. She did once try it on with me. Caused herself a hernia, I suspect, and dropped me after lifting me only a few inches from my snooze in the fields.'

'Can't be very intelligent, trying to pick up a tortoise!' Patty Two said with a smirk.

Isabella began to smile at the funny picture this friendly butterfly had just conjured in her head, and almost burst into laughter at one point when she imagined this tortoise bouncing on a springy tuft of grass from a few inches up in the air.

'Did the bump hurt?' the little fox asked.

'Not really,' Mabel said. 'I quite enjoyed the bounce. I tried to ask her to do it again but, when I turned around, she had disappeared quietly on her silent wings.

'I have seen many foxes and have some as friends,' Mabel went on, after a few moments of further coat-shaking by the little fox. 'In fact, you don't look like a fennec fox at all. You look more like an ordinary fox. As far as I am aware, fennecs live in much hotter climates where there are lots of sandy deserts, and they have very pale colours. You have . . . not.'

'I have an acquaintance that is—' Patty Two began to speak.

A mellow voice washed over them. 'Hello, you two,' it said.

'Poppy!' Mabel cried out, with joy in her voice. 'How lovely to see you again. What brings you to this neck of the woods?'

'I heard from a close friend that you had come across a needy little fox cub who might wish for some company and a bit of friendship. Do I see that she is partial to bramble-bush sitting?' Poppy the older fox said.

'Dropped from a *moderate* height into *this* bush by—' Patty Two tried to explain.

'A rather large eagle owl, by any chance?' Poppy butted in.

'Yes! Yes! That's what it was!' little Isabella shouted, joyful that she could finally remember what had happened to her.

Patty Two continued to explain this little fox's history, to increasing surprise and growing elation on Poppy's whiskery, foxy face.

'Before you go any further, my friend, my aunt tells me that one of her *six* cubs disappeared a while ago and—' Poppy said.

'Would she have been called Bella, by any chance?' Isabella slipped quietly into the conversation.

Silence ambushed the group, forcing all three to turn to look at this little fox cub intently.

'Indeed she would!' Poppy gasped quietly. 'Her missing daughter was – *is* – called . . . Isabella, and we had a feeling she might have been taken by the afore-mentioned eagle owl.'

'Thank you, Foxy Poppy,' Isabella said gratefully. 'You have just fitted the missing pieces of my lost jigsaw into place. Now I can remember everything. My three older brothers and I were playing at running up and down a hill – well, I was *crawling* up and down, to be more accurate, for my part. I had just about reached the sunny, warm bit at the top when I realised that I could no longer feel the grassy earth under my paws. However, I *could* feel the *wind* blowing through my fur. The drop into this . . . uncomfortable and prickly bed is the *second* time recently that I have been picked up and dropped, too. The next thing I felt *this* time was a scratch to my eye, and all those thorns in my fur holding me down so I couldn't move.'

'Well, I do declare, Mabel Tortoise and Patty Two Butterfly, that I believe you have found my long-lost cousin,' Poppy Fox gasped with delight. 'My Aunt Bella will be so pleased.'

Chapter 12

'Have you ever thought—?' Patty Two asked as they took a well-earned rest in a shallow cave in the Painted Hills.

'Only when I have had my dinner and a good sit down,' Mabel butted in once she had become settled and comfortable in a deeply aromatic hollow of dry grasses.

'What might have happened to our new friends we have helped along our travels had we not become involved in their lives?' Patty Two said, ignoring her good friend's interruption. 'You do remember them all, I assume?'

'Of course I do!' Mabel harrumphed sharply. 'Tortoises *do* have the most amazing memory of *all* creatures, don't forget. Now, what were you saying?'

Patty Two smiled, never sure whether she fully understood Mabel's rather strange sense of humour. Quite often you had to wait a little longer for the punchline, and by that time you had usually forgotten what she had started to say anyway.

'Which one was your favourite, my dear friend?' Patty Two asked, not sure whether she would receive an answer from her deep-thinking comrade-in-arms.

'No favourites.' Mabel's quick response took her completely by surprise. 'I have enjoyed bringing peace and tranquillity to them all. They are all good souls who had become a little lost on their journey forward and—'

'Ssh!' Patty Two almost hissed as she puffed out her tiny face in warning to her friend. Then she whispered, 'Someone is clumping through those trees by the waterfall.'

'Hellooo!' a deeply resonant voice boomed through the entrance to the clearing leading to the cave. 'Er . . . anybody there?'

Mabel moved slowly out of the cave to take a look at who might be needing their help, but saw nothing in the clearing at all.

'Nothing there,' she said as Patty Two joined her, alighting on her carapace.

'Try looking at the tall oak tree close to the rock face to our left,' Patty Two suggested. 'Can you see what looks like a very tall pair of raggy . . . ears?'

'I see,' Mabel agreed. 'Looks like a rather large something or other . . . Hello!' she yelled. 'You, up there! You can come into our clearing if you wish. We don't bite . . . well, not at first, anyway.'

After a moment or two, a rather large, tall, very thin and unkempt brown bear stepped very slowly sideways from behind the tree. Dark bushy brows almost covered the creature's piercing, close-together eyes, atop a snout that bore dried-on food around its mouth that seemed to have been there for some time.

It was fortunate that Mabel's neck was flexible, because *this* bear was taller than any creature she had seen before.

'Would you mind coming closer and sitting down?' Mabel asked calmly, as if it was a common thing to have big bears stumbling into your space. 'You see, it's making my neck ache looking up to you.'

'Er . . . yes,' the bear mumbled as it moved forward, tripped over an almost invisible tree root and tumbled to the floor, not three paces from the tortoise.

'Good to see you. Welcome,' Mabel greeted the bear without batting an eyelid. 'My name's Mabel. And this is my friend, Patty Two.'

'But there's only one of them, and I know it is a butterfly, because I have seen quite a lot of them at times,' the bear answered, sitting back on its haunches, a smile seemingly beginning to grow.

Gracious! What big, sharp teeth it had!

'My name is Gracie, and I am a brown bear,' the bear continued, realising too late that this was obvious, as she stood up and sat down again quickly, causing the ground to shake alarmingly and Patty Two to flutter up from her friend's shell.

'Sorry about that,' Gracie said apologetically. 'Not in control of my actions sometimes. "Clumsy," my mother used to say before she and my Pappy were kidnapped.'

'Kidnapped?' Patty Two puzzled. 'How do you mean?'

'They were both captured, put in a large crate by humans and taken away,' Gracie explained. 'I was playing with some friends in a nearby wood and was left on my own.'

'That's dreadful,' Mabel snapped. 'It shouldn't be allowed.'

'"Humans are allowed to do most things where wild creatures are concerned," my nanny used to say,' Gracie added sadly. 'I just wish I had my mother and father here with me. It would be so much fun, and we all would be happier, I'm sure.'

'Zoo,' Patty Two said.

'Bless you!' Mabel retorted. 'That's a bad cold you have there.'

'No,' Patty Two said in return. 'A zoo is a place where humans keep wild creatures so that *other* humans can watch them.'

'Why would they want to do that?' Gracie the bear asked, puzzled why that was the case – *if* it was the case. 'They could come and see us here if they wanted to.'

'No idea,' the tortoise returned, unable to understand any creature that would want to capture another so they could . . . look at it. 'I think that happened to my Uncle Tony, who lived on an island somewhere far, far away.'

'Most humans can be very understanding, friendly and helpful,' Patty Two observed. 'If they were all like that, the whole world would be a much better place, and we would all get along just fine. I'm sure it *will* happen – one day. Until then, I hope *you*, Gracie Bear, will join us here to enjoy your life with friends who like you and will help you when you need it.'

'Deal!' Gracie uttered a friendly growl as she danced around, tripped on a dead tree root and fell over with a bump, smiling very broadly, grateful that she had finally come across creatures she could relate to.

Chapter 13

Jet Black was a creature of legend within the Misty Wood – a large feline who rarely left her comfortable den at the foot of Mount Freedom where the warm waters of River Tolerance cascaded from an underground flow into open river once again. She had been here in these woods for many years, where her mate had lived and where their offspring had joined this world. She had borne only one cub because her mate had died trying to protect his family against a rogue pride of errant lions from the plains.

Now her youngster had disappeared, too. How cruel life could be when there was no one who cared whether you were alive or not.

'Stop!' Jet Black snarled as an unwanted, uninvited and very strange creature lumbered into her domain. 'You are not wanted here. You—'

'Good morning, Alya,' the creature said as she slowed to a halt before the mysterious feline.

'How do you know my name?' the feline spat out in a warning hiss.

'I saw it scratched into a tree's bark just down the path,' the newcomer replied. 'That *is* your name, isn't it?'

'And you are—?' the feline asked sharply.

'I am a tortoise called Mabel,' the visitor explained. 'I heard that you have lost both mate and offspring in reasonably quick succession. I am here to help.'

'What do you think *you* can achieve when *I* have hunted high and low for my little kitten, Ashe, to no avail?' Jet Black scoffed. 'Tortoise, you say? What can a slow-moving creature like you, who bears a thick and very heavy shell, do when someone like me has been able to achieve . . . nothing?'

'I am not saying that I *will* be able to better your efforts, but I have a magical friend who might,' Mabel went on. 'At least let us try.'

'Please come inside my abode, out of the rain,' the black feline suggested. 'Although with *your* construction, rain would be the last thing to cause you problems.'

'Cosy, comfortable cave you have here,' the tortoise observed as she was led inside, to see plenty of dry bedding straw, two carcasses of some indeterminate creatures hanging about in the depths of the cave – which was reasonably warm for the home of a warm-blooded creature – and a gently gurgling small stream flowing through, disappearing underground close to the cave's entrance.

'I see you read the tree, then?' Jet Black said once they were settled.

'Couldn't miss it,' Mabel said. 'Even at my height. Why?'

'It is my "given" name, bestowed upon me by my mother at birth,' the feline explained in her silkily deep rumble. 'A name handed down through successive families for the firstborn, whether female or male. The name I am *known* by is Jet Black.'

Mabel could understand why this feline was both feared and revered at the same time. Only recognisable in the dark by her green eyes and her sharp white teeth, she had become an awesome predator that no other creature could see or hear approaching. Deadly.

'Do you live alone through choice?' Mabel asked quietly, not wishing to be too intrusive or inquisitive. 'Or is there some other – more personal – reason?'

Jet Black lay without moving or blinking, a quiet purring rumble resonating in her throat as she breathed almost in silence.

'My mate had heard that a rogue pride of lions had moved into our territory and was about to clear out all other felines in the area,' Jet Black began quietly, sharp memories obviously governing her tale. 'He went out with several others to drive them away, and I never saw him again. It wasn't much longer after that when my little kitten, Ashe, disappeared too. I spent a long time searching for both, combing every inch of our hunting and living grounds, to no avail. That is when I realised they were no more and decided to move here to spend my time in solitude with my thoughts and memories.'

'You have obviously been in pain and have suffered a great deal of anguish throughout your trials,' Mabel said sympathetically.

'No one deserves to have such a degree of mental suffering thrust upon them.'

'That is very true.' A new, softer voice joined the gathering, as a gloriously coloured butterfly landed on Mabel's carapace, just above her head.

The feline stiffened, ready to pounce should this new intruder prove to be more dangerous than she appeared.

'No need to become agitated, my dear,' Mabel soothed. 'This is a good friend. As you can see, she is a butterfly, and she is called—'

'Patty Two at your service, Alya Jet Black,' the butterfly announced.

'Getting to be very busy in here,' the feline snarled, raising her hackles as she crouched a little lower, seeming to be ready to pounce. 'Anyone else in your entourage?'

'As it happens,' Patty Two answered soothingly, 'I have someone I should like you to meet.'

Her words were drowned by a frighteningly loud and threatening roar just outside the front entrance to the cave which almost deafened the two companions.

That roar had a startling effect on the resident feline. Her head lifted, her ears twitched to home in on the sound, and her unblinking eyes opened wide in shock and surprise. A larger black feline with a white dusting to the chest strode through the entrance and leapt over the stream to land next to the female. She had recognised that roar in an instant, standing to rub cheeks in heartfelt greeting to her missing mate.

'How can this be true?' she stammered. 'I was convinced I had lost you.'

'After the conflict with the lions, some of us had been seriously injured almost to the point of death,' the male explained, his deep voice rumbling in his throat. 'It took a long time, but once I recovered I set out to find you, but to no avail. You had moved on. Guess what I did find, though.'

A startling mewing and high-pitched squeaking interrupted his explanation, as a young, speckled feline leapt onto the two adults.

'Ashe! My kitten!' Jet Black screeched. Until this overwhelmingly emotional moment, she had not believed she would ever see her daughter again. 'I never believed in my wildest dreams that this could happen!'

The family rolled together, hugging and snuffling as feline families do, welcoming each other back into the life they once shared and enjoyed.

'I need to thank you from the bottom of my gruff old heart, Patty Two – and your sound companion,' the male feline said as he turned towards them. 'You will never know—'

His grateful words fell on deaf ears as he gasped his surprise into an empty cave entrance. Patty Two and Mabel had spirited themselves away so as not to disturb those wonderful moments of family rebirth.

'Now I know what it means to have friends who will do

whatever it takes to reassure and support others,' Jet Black purred as they all snuggled together to smooth away all their recent hurt and sadness.

Frank English
Author

Born in 1946 in the West Riding of Yorkshire's coal fields around Wakefield, he attended grammar school, where he enjoyed sport rather more than academic work. After three years at teacher training college in Leeds, he became a teacher in 1967. He spent a lot of time during his teaching career entertaining children of all ages, a large part of which was through telling stories, and encouraging them to escape into a world of imagination and wonder; for example, he found some of his most disturbed youngsters to be very talented poets. He has always had a wicked sense of humour, which has blossomed only during the time he has spent with his wife, Denise. This sense of humour also allowed many youngsters to survive often difficult and brutalising home environments.

In 2006, he retired after forty years working in schools with young people who had significantly disrupted lives because of behaviour disorders and poor social adjustment, generally brought about through circumstances beyond their control. At the same time as he moved from leafy-lane, suburban, middle-class school teaching in Leeds to residential schooling for emotional and behavioural disturbance in the early 1990s, changed family circumstances provided the spur for Frank to achieve his ambitions. Supported by his wife, Denise, he achieved a Master's degree in his mid-forties and a PhD at the age of fifty-six, because he had always wanted to do so.

Now enjoying glorious retirement, he spends as much time as life will allow writing, reading and travelling.

Other children's books Frank has written to date:

Magic Parcel: The Awakening	Published June 2010
Magic Parcel: The Gathering Storm	Published March 2011
Magic Parcel: A New Dawn	Published August 2012
18 Mulberry Road	Published September 2011
25 Primrose Walk	Published January 2013

Autumn Adventures	Published September 2013
Winter Tales	Published September 2014
Towards Spring	Published September 2016
Juniper's Tale	Published August 2018
Honey	Published January 2019
The Story of Lemuel Pecker	Published April 2019
Josephine's Journey	Published June 2019
Holly's Prize	Published April 2020
Garnett's Grand Getaway	Published May 2020
Sara's Astonishing Story	Published June 2020
The Boys in Black	Published August 2020
The Magic Whistle and the Tiny Bag of Wishes	Published October 2020
Half Moon Farm	Published March 2021
The Spirit Tree	Published March 2022